"CAPTIVATING CANVEY"

Residents' Guidebook

or

How to get to Canvey Heights

Edited and designed
by Lucy Harrison
2007

CANVEY GUIDES was a project by Lucy Harrison in 2007.

As well as this book the project incorporates the Rendezvous Walking Club and an audio guide, which can be hired from Canvey Library or downloaded from www.canveyguides.com
Canvey Guides is part of 'Art U Need; An Outdoor Revolution', curated by Bob & Roberta Smith and managed by Commissions East.

Captivating Canvey; Residents' Guidebook
Published by Rendezvous Press ISBN 978-0-9555400-0-4
© Lucy Harrison 2007
Texts © the authors 2006–7
Captivating Canvey was the name of a guidebook first published on Canvey in 1927 by B.A. McCave and continued by F.B. McCave until 1974 (see above)
All opinions stated are those of the individual writers and not of any organisation
Information provided is anecdotal or personal opinion and at times may not be historically accurate

Front cover sign painted by Canvey signwriter Bob 'The Brush' Gibbons, and held by walkers at the February 2007 Rendezvous Club.
Book design by Lucy Harrison
Photographs © Lucy Harrison unless otherwise indicated
Annotated maps by pupils in Applied Arts at Castle View School
Texts in italics were transcribed from interviews

Copy editors: Sharon Kivland (book) and Inna Ward (audio guide)
Design consultants: Steve Parker and Manuela Wyss
Assistance with transcription: Rachel Mckeown
Printed at Aldgate Press
www.canveyguides.com

★ CONTENTS ★

Preface	5
How to get to Canvey	9
Walk no. 1 via Rainbow Road	10
Walk No. 2 via the High Street	12
2nd Hand Rose	16
Captain Birdseye and Old Benson	20
The Arcade by Steve Bullock	22
The Settlement by Graham Stevens	24
The Catwoman	26
Houses Sheds & Caravans by David Offley	28
Walk No. 3 via the sea wall	32
Incident on Long Road by Roger Esgrove	34
Haystack Corner	35
Arthur Reed and Roman George	36
Oz Now– You Next by Jim Gray	38
The 39 Cafe by Shirley Coates	40
The Rio Cinema by Kevin Gardner	41
Detour: Thorney Bay– Joan Liddiard, Chris Keene and Irene Willis	43
The Casino by David Cain	47
Canvey Point	52
The Concrete Barge by David Bullock & Andrew Jackson	54
Canvey Heights	57
The View to Leigh by Margaret Payne	60
The View Towards the Creek by Chris Fenwick	61
Lee Brilleaux's pirate map	62
Lunch at the Tip by Barbara Taylor	64
Fond Memories of Canvey Tip by Janet Penn	65
Around Canvey Heights	
A Walk by Valerie Lynch	66
Tewkes Road by George Beecham	67
Tewkes Road by Derek Lynch	68
Newlands Park, Amada and Killoran by Alan Piper	69
Footpaths of Canvey by Valerie Lynch	70
Miscellaneous	71
Acknowledgements	79

Do you ever visit Canvey Heights at all?
Canvey Heights? where's that?
You know the old tip, and Kings Camp?
Oh yeah, yeah, I know the tip, I know Kings...
Well its there, Canvey tip is now Canvey Heights
Is it?

Interview with a local resident, August 2006

PREFACE

THIS BOOK will show you the way to Canvey Heights. It will also invite you to make the most of the other public – and not so public – spaces of Canvey Island along the way, as recommended by your tour guides, a group of Canvey residents who have chosen locations to be included here.

THIS BOOK IS FOR

1. Long term residents
2. Recent arrivals
3. Visitors & day trippers
4. Ex-pats
5. Anyone else

Although laid out as a series of walks, occasionally there will be a 'detour' which goes off the track or is not part of the main walk. Also interspersed are stories related to characters indelibly linked in people's minds to certain places, and who are described with affection. It should be noted that this book celebrates people's memories and anecdotes, and is not intended as a historical guide.

A number of these books will be distributed as part of a 'new residents' pack' by Fisks Estate Agents, to people moving to the island.

How to get to Canvey

For non-island residents, Canvey can be reached by train to Benfleet, or by road via the A13 east towards Southend-on-sea, then the A130 south onto the island.

As you cross the bridge on the A130 you will see 'JULIE 4 LEN' on your left.

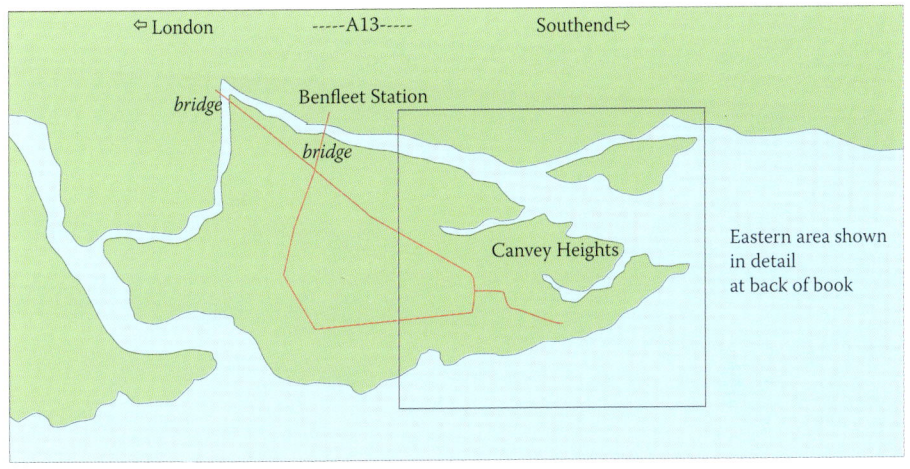

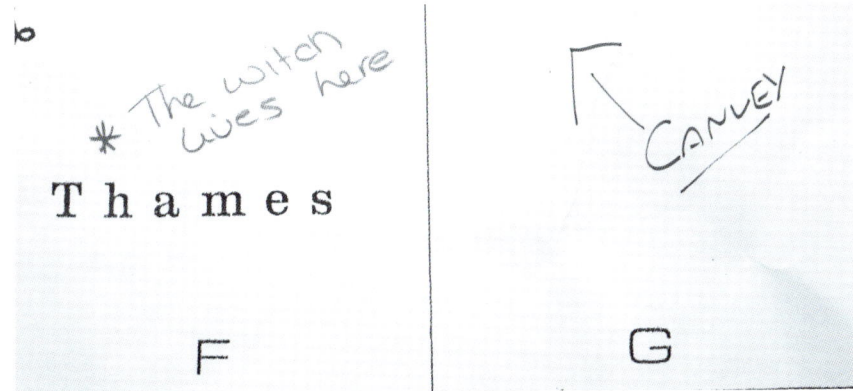

Walk no. 1: From the town centre to Canvey Heights via Rainbow Road

Duration: 25 minutes
Terrain: mostly pavement until Canvey Heights
Aesthetic: fairly dull but the most direct route

Brief directions: Go up Larup Avenue from the High Street and along Rainbow Road. Cross over the road and head up the concrete pathway with Kings Park on your left and the playing field on your right.

Reproduced by permission of the Essex Record Office

If you go this way you will walk past the site of the original Rendezvous Club (above) whose namesake is mentioned on page 74, and its replacement, the Rainbow Club. The location of the Rendezvous Club is disputed: often placed on Larup Avenue, the daughters of the Went family who co-managed the club believe it to have been on Waalwyk Drive, on your left at the junction of Rainbow Road. The Rainbow Club was near the site of number 12 Larup Avenue.

Note as you go past Mitchells Avenue that there is a new pathway that has been made by children fetching balls through the hole in the fence (left).

You will also pass the entrance to Kings Park Village and will be able to look over the fence at the private bungalows there.

When you have reached Canvey Heights, turn to page 57.

WALK NO. 2: THE HIGH STREET

Duration: 45 minutes
Terrain: mostly pavement with the last section possibly muddy
Aesthetic: mostly residential streets with a varied selection of stories

Brief directions: From the town centre go all the way along the High Street past the library and Sainsbury's. Carry on past Small Gains Corner, with the option of a detour up Baardwyck Avenue, past the Canvey Club, the Transport Museum and Leigh Beck School. When you get to Canvey Supply and a roundabout, turn left past a gate and go up to the sea wall. You will see Kings Park in front of you and as you come down from the sea wall the gates of Canvey Heights will be in front of you.

Your tour guides for this walk are Stephen Bullock, David Cain, Terry Hull, Derek Lynch, David Offley, Margaret Payne, John Pring, and Graham Stevens.

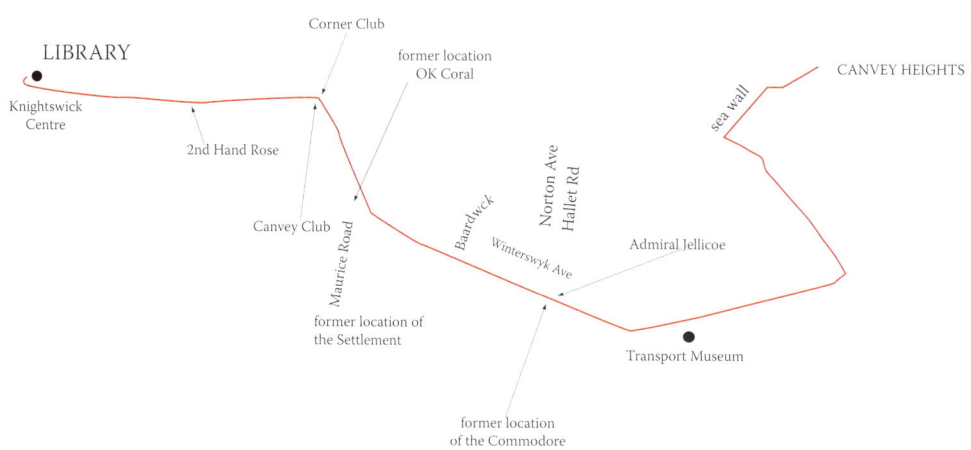

Walk with Knightswick Centre to your right and as you pass Sainsbury's, continue straight ahead at the fork in road (also signposted towards Canvey Island FC), noticing as you do the shop names to your left: *Del Boys Cards, Kerry-Anne's, Pick and Choose, Pining for You, Fireman's Relief Aid, Care and Share, Tower Radio.*

There is a rumour that Tower Radio wanted to start a radio station in the 1960s called Radio Tower. It was supposedly going to be transmitted from the mouth of the Thames. They also used to hire out prams of all different sizes to holiday makers.

DEREK LYNCH
The original Tower Radio stores, it was still where that one is now, at the top there, but run by Mr and Mrs Shofrun, and I used to take our accumulators down there; they were a glass battery and she used to put them on charge for fivepence or sevenpence and I used to take another one to connect to our radio. She also used to hire out prams, all down the side she had folding prams and big prams, and when people came down on holiday they used to hire them out for the children.

After about ten minutes you will pass May Avenue on your right and the War Memorial on your left. Shortly after *Enchanted Moments* at the corner of May Avenue, you will see a row of shops in old buildings. The carpet shop is housed in the former building of the Kynochs club. You should be able to see the old sign underneath the present one.

OPEN

ART U NEED: AN OUTDOOR REVOLUTION
CANVEY GUIDES

www.canveyguides.com

Canvey Guides is a project by artist Lucy Harrison and is:

1. The Rendezvous Walking Club. Meets at 2pm on the first Sunday of every month at the corner of Canvey Heights. All welcome - maps, itineraries and suggested topics of conversation provided.

2. An audio guide and guide book to be produced in March 2007, which will outline a series of walks taking in residents' points of interest, which so far include disappeared buildings, old pieces of graffiti and sites of first kisses. Anyone can contribute - it's not an official history, it's about how people feel about Canvey.

CONTRIBUTE BY: BEING A TOUR GUIDE AT THE RENDEZVOUS CLUB / BEING A READER ON THE AUDIO GUIDE / WRITING A DESCRIPTION OF AN EVENT AT A LOCATION / SENDING IN PHOTOS OR DRAWINGS / OR JUST COME ALONG TO THE RENDEZVOUS CLUB- FIRST SUNDAY OF THE MONTH, 2PM, CANVEY HEIGHTS

DEADLINE FOR CONTRIBUTIONS: 10TH FEBRUARY 2007

You can email us administrator@canveyguides.com or phone Lucy on 07927 963666 or post to Lucy Harrison c/o Canvey Library for more info see www.canveyguides.com

ART U NEED

At the end of this row of shops is one called *2nd Hand Rose*. It is run by Frank who makes roundabouts and boats with moving parts from rubbish, and keeps them in the back of the shop. If you visit the shop, you can ask Frank if he will show you the models. He is sometimes a bit shy but perhaps rather flattered that you are taking an interest in his work.

An item bought in *2nd Hand Rose* would be an ideal souvenir from your High Street walk.

18

aptain Birdseye

THE HIGH STREET is the area where a man known as Captain Birdseye would often be seen walking between the Point and the Haystack.

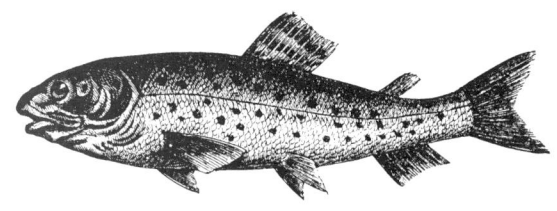

DAVID CAIN: Captain Birdseye, Barnacle Bill, Captain Birdseye we used to call him That was just his name, that was all, he just used to wander around. It'd be summer, wouldn't it? It'd be a heat wave, you're talking a real, real heat wave. We're talking about a hundred degrees, hundred and ten. And he would be out with a sou'wester on, and big black carrier bags wandering up the road with Wellington boots on.

JOHN PRING: He was nothing to do with the sea at all as far as I am aware... but he did used to wander around in boots yellow things and yes the sou'wester... He lived in one of the roads off Point Road in a– oh it was a dreadful place, He was just a sad... he was ever such a nice guy, but not quite– I don't know how you'd describe it really, but the kind of person that children would make fun of, and throw stones at his house, and things like that– you know that kind of – it is sad really, people are very cruel. Anyway we knew him, and one of my jobs in life was to sort him out and he decided that he wanted to leave Canvey and live in the country, and we sold his property for him although that didn't help because he had nowhere to go, and in the end we found a mobile home site, just the other side of Stock in Chelmsford, on Baker's Lane, there's a kind of mobile home site which is in the middle of the country, in the woods, and this guy said he wanted to live there, and I can remember taking him in my car over there and sorting out the mobile home and organising for him to move. It's difficult to understand– he just wasn't quite the ticket or whatever– there was nothing wrong with him for goodness sake, he just didn't fit into the modern world. He lived in Canvey happily for years– everyone knew him because he just used to walk up and down– he walked up to the High Street and back again, and now and again– well, he must be dead now– but every now and then, because I live in Stock now, I used to see him at the bus stop, waiting to catch a bus somewhere– still dressed the same.

CONTINUE ALONG THE HIGH STREET. Continue past the bus stop, Oxford Road, *Kitchen Craft Bedrooms*, Mitchells Avenue and a petrol station on the left. In front of you, you'll be able to see *Sandwich Bar, Tudor Motors, Stop and Shop*, and on the right the Canvey Club, with its outdoor toilet visible to the left. The road bends to the right– this is Small Gains Corner. *Tudor Bargain Store*, like Aladdin's cave. *Trade Fireworks*. Arcadia Road on the right, *Phoenix Food Stores*, former *Granary Stores* on the left, opposite Maurice Road on the right.

Stop at the junction of Maurice Road.

OLD BENSON

TERRY HULL: There was a famous man. Old Benson. He used to go and play the trombone. Busker up town. Well he used to bunk in the Rio Cinema through the window, round the side. And he said "Right, give us a bunk up and put..." And he got stuck so we went and got the manager and said "There's a bloke trying to bunk in.!"
DAVID CAIN: Did he have a caravan at Small Gains Corner?
TH: No, I don't think so. I'm not quite sure.
DC: Well someone had a caravan at Small Gains Corner. Like a Gypsy one. And when he died - this is true - when he died, they found loads of money in his mattress. He used to stuff all the money in the mattress. His name was Benson.
TH: Yeah. He was a busker. He used to go up London by train and make a few quid. He got this great big trombone with him. Big thing to you know, to pull about.

The Arcade: The High Street
(opposite the Clockhouse)
Stephen Bullock

To the left (east) side of the house 198 High Street, a converted newsagent's, ran an alleyway that led to an arcade with a varied selection of shops. Due to its 'wild west' appearance with a raised wooden walkway it became known locally as the 'OK Coral'. It was rumoured to have been blue and white as traces of paint could be seen on the woodwork, the shop windows were always due to be cleaned tomorrow.

The corner of land between the Arcade and Maurice Road was a large muddy car park so there was always somewhere to park between the large puddles and flood siren for the shoppers.

The first shop, the most remembered, was called *The Gun Shop*. The window display of targets and other gun-related items prevented you from seeing inside so it was always a mystery what guns were for sale inside. I used to stand by the door waiting for someone to go in or out so I could peek in but got "MOVE OUT THE WAY SON", so I never did get to see what guns they sold inside.

The next shop was a women's hair salon. Describing inside this shop is also a problem for me as the windows were frosted at the bottom and being small, I couldn't see in. By the time I'd be tall enough to peer in, the arcade would be long gone. All I can say is there were pictures of various hair styles in the windows as that's all I saw.

The next shop was Selby's the barbers which was made famous when Canvey's very own 'Dr Feelgood' band had their photograph taken outside for the cover of their album *Malpractice*. The interior of this shop, unfortunately, is known by me as I can remember sitting in the barber's chair hearing the question "What do you want son?" No matter what you replied, you ended up staring in the mirror watching all your hair being cut off and swept into a hole in the floor. You then walked outside ready to join the army! Not only was it cheap but you only needed it cut once a year... but would it grow again?

The next two shops had various vendors; each time I'd visit it seemed to be different one. The arcade then 'dog-legged' in a south-east direction, perhaps a devious plan to display their wares to the approaching shoppers?

The next shop was at first a mystery to me as I couldn't see in due to the frosted glass. Unfortunately one day I wiped the window with my white shirt sleeve which turned black. It wasn't frosted glass but a protective layer of years of grime and dirt. When I peered in, to my horror the bench up against the windows was covered in false teeth and gums, thousands of them mostly hiding in the dust. That was the day I started to clean my teeth daily as I now knew where the false teeth came from and they weren't going in my mouth! As the years went on, the pile of teeth and gums seemed to grow higher; did anyone on Canvey wear these false teeth? I never wiped the window again but had great delight in getting other astonished friends to peer in – ha ha!

The last shop in the arcade finished its days as a second hand car parts shop. As a schoolboy my paper round money would pay for one item at a time, I thought I could build my own car a bit at a time. I asked my mate John if he ever built the car and I think he made a record about it.

The 'OK Coral' never boasted major trade and in the early 1980s the car park got covered in houses and the arcade disappeared under them. The only old building left here is opposite Maurice Road, the wooden 'Granary' building.

The question is, where did all the false teeth go?

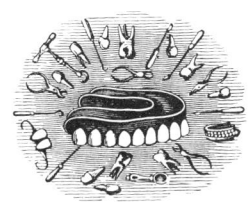

Detour: The Settlement
Graham Stevens

Walk down Maurice Road until you reach the junction with Crescent Road

We're in Maurice Road at the moment, about 150 yards south of the junction with Crescent Road, and we're on the site of the so-called Wilberforce bungalow, which was on the east side of Maurice Road. In 1907, this particular piece of land, which is now occupied by four 4-bedroom houses, between Maurice Road and Lottem Road, was bought by my great-grandmother Sarah Stevens. At the time she was living in London, in the Clapham area, and wanted to buy a holiday retreat on Canvey Island. She was also a lady of very strong religious convictions and knew the connections between William Wilberforce and a property called Battersea Rise House, which was about to be pulled down in 1905. This house was the meeting place of the Clapham Sect, who were motivating the cause of the abolition of slavery. With the disposal of the property in Battersea Rise, my great-grandmother was able to go to an auction and buy various building materials and interiors that were part of the property. In particular this included the library, which was designed by Pitt the Younger. So these various bits of building material which included panels from the library, windows and even a stone eagle, were transported by horse and cart to Canvey, and were installed in about 1908 by my great-grandfather with the help of a local carpenter, and my grandfather who was probably in his early 20s at that time, and they built the bungalow on this site.

They called the property The Settlement. *At some time an oval plaque was made up and this contains the information about the panelling and the floor of the library from Battersea Rise House which were laid in the property, and that is in the Heritage Centre. And also the sole survivor other than the plaque is the eagle and he is still in residence on the island with the Stevens family. Eventually the family moved and took the name* The Settlement *to their next property.*

Walk down Crescent Road to the end.

As you turn at the junction of Maurice Road you might have noticed that the road itself wasn't straight, there was a little twist in it, and that was because we're on a dividing line between the two different estates, and the little twist in the road is because none of the estate roads actually lined up with each other, and Maurice Road was the first one to be metalled. And then looking at Crescent Road it's changed in its appearance as far as the centre is concerned because this was the ditch right the way down the middle and this was the border between the two farms. Looking over to our left hand side over there, Weel Road, I recall down there was the famous Canvey hotel, which was a large green building and I think it was used for rental accommodation for families. Looking up towards the east end of Crescent Road, on the left hand side there's a rather odd shaped building, well that is a conversion of Iris Stores, which was in our day known as Miss Hunt's, and

it was a general stores, and it had lots of little toys in it, and I remember looking at lead soldiers, and rather crude cars which were probably the post war version of a Dinky toy. I know my sister bought her first doll there. You have to imagine this next bit because you can't walk through there any more but you could walk through there round the back of Iris Stores, through onto the church site, which is St Anne's church, and that was on a kind of mound, and then it ran down towards the ditch, and there was the bridge, and I think it was the place for teenage escapades. And if you go round the corner... you see this bit of unmade road here, that is the remnants of a flood road. It's a peculiarity that this supposedly unadopted road and that little bit remains as it was just after the flood.

If we were standing at the time of the property being built, we'd be standing in a field with no possibilities of any other properties at all. We'd be looking at the sea wall there and as we can see down the end of Maurice Road, there would be a much smaller sea wall and we'd be able to look right to the Point. And seeing open fields all around us.

The Catwoman lived in various places around leigh beck

One of the most well-known characters of Canvey, the Catwoman would wander the Leigh Beck area wearing brown clothes and pushing a pram full of cats, all dressed in bonnets. The Catwoman, often wrongly rumoured to be related to a Radio 1 DJ with the same surname, led a sorry existence living on the donations of kind Canvey residents and the cats were taken away after allegations of cruelty.

Go back to the High Street and continue on the walk to the East.

You'll pass the *Admiral Jellicoe* pub on your left, and Seaview Road, where the Commodore used to be, on your right. Shortly after this you will see Leigh Beck School and the Transport Museum. There is a park bench on the left hand side of the road. If you need a rest, stop here and look at the view of the houses opposite.

Castle Point Transport Museum
105 Point Road
Canvey Island SS8

Housing the Eastern National Collection

Open the first and third Sunday of every month, 10am – 5pm
Admission free, but donations welcome

www.freewebs.com/transportmuseum

Houses, sheds and Caravans
David Offley

When I got out of Great Ormond Street, they sent me back to my parents, and I had plaster all the way up my legs, right? And I must have sat on my mother's hat, because she had one of those hats with pins. She came home and she went into a terrific rage, because she could, couldn't she, once she went, she really did go, and she kicked me from the top of the stairs down to the bottom, and that's when they took me away and put me in the crippled children's home, to get me away from my mother. I came out of the home, and they never had anywhere to put me, and so they put me in this Borstal. It was meant to be for a matter of a week. Right, it ended up being three years.

Sheila, my sister, she heard I was coming home from the Borstal from my mother. She was fostered in the hotel at the bottom of Seaview Road. There used to be a hotel down there, and she was fostered in that, with a few other children. And she used to walk down Seaview Road, and my mother and father had two rooms at the top of Mr and Mrs Petty's house. They had two rooms at the top there, and actually Tony knew me very well from when I was small, and they actually ended up managing to get a place in Norton Avenue which was two sheds and a pantechnicon caravan, and get me out. And that was what we lived in. Actually I believe it was two sheds and a lavatory. We slept in the pantechnicon caravan, one of the sheds was our front room, and the other was the kitchen, and then the toilet, and they rented it for a pound a week.

Well, my sister, she never knew she had a brother. She never knew she had a brother! And when she heard that she had a brother, straight away she turned round and said, "Can he box?" And they said yeah, he's been boxing in the home and that, and that was all she thought about because she had to wear glasses, and all the kids were calling her "four eyes:. And what happened was, she went to Leigh Beck school, with Miss Vincent, and when I was first going up to the gate, all I could hear was "fight, fight, fight, fight", and I thought God what's happening here? And it was the first time I'd been to school, I'd never been to school in my life. And I walked in the gate, and this boy, I think it's one of the Slaters, was coming up towards me, and I thought, "Christ what's going on?" And he said "Your sister reckons you're going to beat the hell out of me because I pinched her milk." In actual fact he came very unstuck, because I'd just come out of a Borstal and they had learnt you to look after yourself, and in the end I done more damage than what I was supposed to do so Miss Vincent was right up here, you know, really having a go at me.

Anyway, because I was dyslexic, and also that I hadn't been taught from the age of five, I was shoved at the back of the class and given plasticine. But I never ever got anyone pick on me, because of them days when my sister said... and it went all the way through, I never got bullied. So in some respects, when I look back on it, I could have cursed Sheila at the time, but she done me a favour, if you know what I mean, because being what they called a dunce, I would have gone through hell, if it wasn't for that, you know. Basically that was how I came to Canvey.

Dad used to get all his furniture for either ten cigarettes or twenty cigarettes from the neighbours, you see. So he turned round and said to the bailiffs, "What about that settee", he said, "it's lovely". and the bailiff said no, no, and he said what do you mean, I paid twenty cigarettes for that! And even today, it makes me laugh, to think he was trying to give stuff to the bailiffs, and they wouldn't have it. In the end they used to walk out and he used to end up going to prison for a weekend or two weeks, but he used to say to me, at first he used to tell me he was going away to work, but as time went on of course I knew, and he used to say, well, it's all right, your mother gets fed, I get three meals a day, which we never used to have at home, and he said I always get the library job, and he didn't mind that, and he used to take the porridge round of a morning, so he didn't mind. I mean, they could do whatever they liked to him, they couldn't hurt him, they couldn't hurt him one bit, because he had had everything they could do to him.

But when we were living in Norton Avenue Dad couldn't pay the rent, and he found that on Hallet Road, there was a – I don't know if you remember this but there was a Missen hut that used to have all shells on it, down there. It used to have all shells, and it used to have a letterbox with shells on it, and that was a Missen hut and two sheds, and we rented that for a pound a week. Now what happened, we were in there and we used to have to get the settees at night and pull them down, but by that time my sister was getting on, and I was getting older, and I actually went down to the Council, and I said to them, because my father and mother, they never had any idea of money, so as I got older, I took over doing the money of the house. What happened was I went to the Council, and I told them, I said, we're all sleeping in one room and we have to pull the beds down and everything, and we need a council house, so I said they have been on the list so I've been told, but they wouldn't take any notice of me, so I said right I'm not going home, and I sat down and there was nothing they could do to move me. So in the end they said we'll send the sanitary inspector round, and so I said yeah, so anyway he came round and when he saw the way we were living, he said you can have 41 West Crescent.

And we got number 41 West Crescent, it's still there today, and when we got it, we had all the bedrooms, and I remember walking in to 41 West Crescent and switching the light on and off, because I thought it was funny having electricity because all the other places we had, we had gas mantles, that you pulled the chains, and you had to be very careful of them. You know, when we moved into West Crescent it was great. But then I remember my mother in West Crescent chucking all my washing out of the top window. And I ended up coming down here to Thissell Road, to a shed, because the Dutchman, now he– I don't know if you've read this but he actually saved forty five lives in the flood. They called him the mad Dutchman, and the reason they called him the mad

Dutchman was he couldn't speak a word of English when he came over, and he was running up and down the wall trying to tell everyone that the sea was coming over, and what he did, he got a dinghy and he actually saved forty five lives. Anyway, when they told him that I had nowhere, he said well you can have that garden shed, but you're not having it for nothing, so he said ten shillings a week, and I said all right, but he put a bed, and electric blanket and he made me quite cosy. But in the morning was the worst bit. I used to get up to do my paper round for Warwicks and I used to do a greengrocer delivery round in the afternoon for Shillams, to earn my money. And in the summer I used to do haymaking, and I remember the bales were so heavy I fell over and hit my head on the wheel. And I got up on the cart at one time to sort something out and they buried me and someone nearly stuck a pitchfork in me. And another thing I used to do, down Kittkatts Road, there used to be a man who had horses, and he used to take the horses up the sea front. And I used to ride them horses up the seafront, I think I got five shillings a week or something like that. And I used to look after pigs for the Jeffries up Winter Gardens way. Anything to earn money. I had to live!

I was fourteen years old at the time, and I was at William Read School, and one of my teachers there was Slasher Hills. I always remember Slasher Hills. He was a smashing bloke. When I was at school we used to call him Slasher Hills and God knows what, but he was the only one who ever taught me anything. He used to sit there and we used to all sit in the class, and he used to sit and look at you, and he always had this book, that he used to read out, and it was about the poachers. And it was a smashing book, smashing story, and when he was teaching you, he used to say, if you used to maybe drift and look out of the window, "Hey! Look at me." And you know he kept you there all the time, very strict he was. I always remember that one time we were having Gardening, and he done something or other to me, I don't know, and I jumped up and put my fists up, so he pulled me out, sent me to the headmaster, but after that he pulled me over one day and he said, "I want you to come to my house". He told me where it was, Rose Road, so I thought hey-ho, what's going to happen, so I went back and he give me a raincoat, a pair of Wellingtons, oh, the things he give me.

I remember I was going through hell at school over uniforms. They started to wear uniforms, and they pulled me in, and Watkins used to pull me out of assembly for a caning, because I had no uniform. I used to get caned regular. And then one day old Slasher Hills he said to me "Why actually do you keep on coming without a uniform?" He said "I can't make it out." So I said "Well, I haven't got one". So he said "Can you get your father to sign a paper so that you get a free uniform?" So I said "I think so," but I was living on Thissell Road, you see, in the shed. And so I got my dad to meet me at the Commodore, down the bottom of Seaview Road, opposite the Admiral Jellicoe. And we met outside and he said to me, "Are you all right, son?" Because he knew what my mother was, you know. Because I remember she told him one day that she was going to leave him, he sparked up straight away and said, "Oh make sure you've got your bus fare!"

When you get to a mini-roundabout and can see *Canvey Supply*, take a sharp left down the short cul-de-sac road, where you will see a rusty gate and bollarded entrance to open land directly ahead.

Walk up the small road, taking care not to trip over the speed bumps. Take the pathway to the right of the gate. You will see a flood gate with the warning sign 'FLOOD GATE KEEP CLEAR'. Continue following the sea wall path and you should eventually see Kings Park, the lake at Small Gains and the gates of Canvey Heights in front of you.

To continue this walk and enter Canvey Heights, turn to page 57.

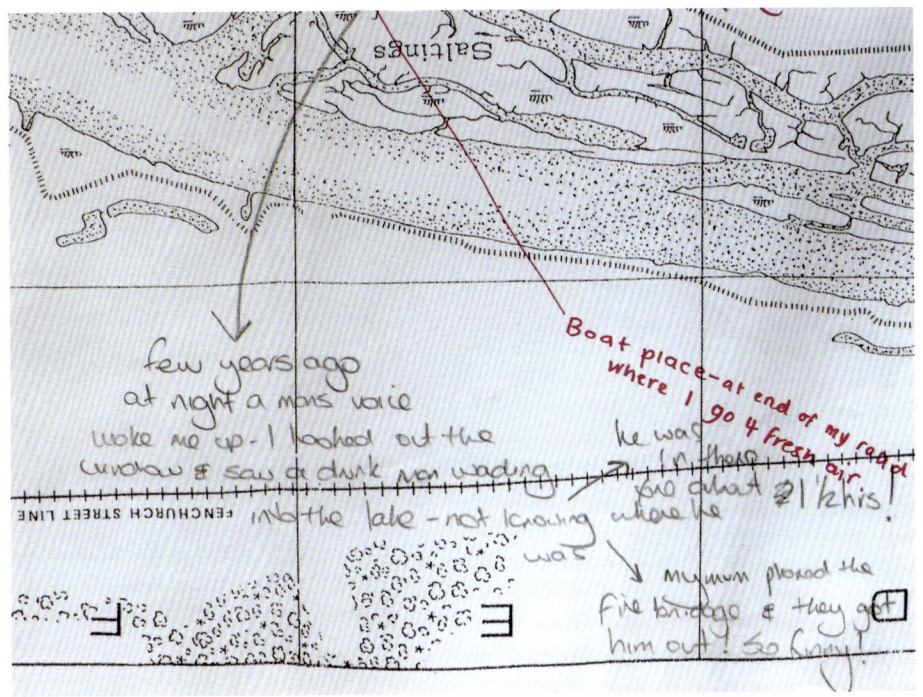

Walk No. 3:
Via the Sea front & the sea wall

Duration: 90 minutes
Terrain: mostly pavement / concrete with muddy sections towards the end
Aesthetic: very scenic with stunning views of the estuary

Brief directions: All the way down Furtherwick Road, optional detour to Thorney Bay then all the way along the sea wall. Up the steps and along the edge of the creek, stopping to look at the Point. Along the rest of the sea wall and down the slope to Canvey Heights.

Your tour guides for this walk are: David Bullock, David Cain, Shirley Coates, Roger Esgrove, Kevin Gardner, Jim Gray, Terry Hull, Andrew Jackson, Chris Keene, Joan Liddiard, Derek Lynch and Irene Willis.

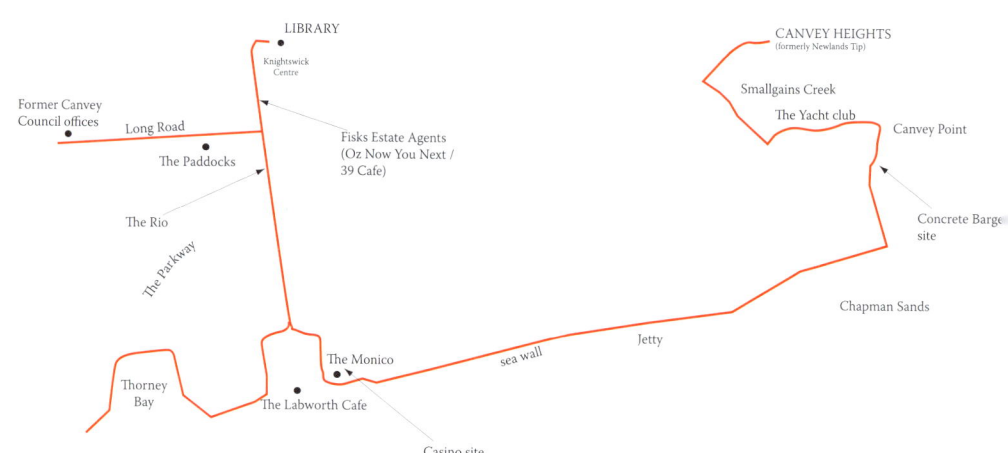

From the library, turn left down Furtherwick Road, past Barclays Bank on your right and Knightswick Shopping Centre on your left. Continue past the entrance to the shopping centre, past *Islanders Fish Bar* and *Grouts Bakers*. Cross the road at the zebra crossing. The *Haystack* pub is on your right, and if you look down Long Road you will be able to see a glimpse of Cisca House and the Paddocks, where Elvis Costello played an impromptu gig in 1979, and where, in an upstairs room, there is a well-hidden projection booth, a leftover from when the hall was a cinema.

If you go further up Long Road you will reach the site of the former Canvey Council building.

Incident on Long Road
Roger Esgrove

I used to be a serving police officer, and I was on duty one nightshift, going on a call to a road accident, when unfortunately, because of the road conditions, I was in a road collision involving an ambulance. It happened at the site of the old council offices which is now the medical centre. We managed to miss the ambulance fortunately, but unfortunately we weren't aware that there were small walls around the garden area with which we collided at a very high speed, causing us to become airborne, and when we did finally come down it created several injuries, multiple injuries, back injuries, neck injuries, broken sternum, for myself and my colleague who was driving suffered facial injuries, back injuries and broken ribs. I was aware that we were airborne because we had gone over the height of the ambulance, and when I actually looked over to the houses, we were level with the first floor windows; we were a long way up. But my main concern at having come down from being airborne, was the fact that I was so pleased to have actually survived the accident but horrified to see the engine starting to smoke, knowing full well that we had taken out the petrol tank and there was petrol all over the place, but unbeknown to me at the time, the fire brigade had actually seen what had happened out of the window and came to our assistance, along with the ambulance crew from the ambulance, and helped us get out of the car. I will be forever grateful to them for actually covering the petrol to prevent it from catching alight, and disconnecting the battery, giving us plenty of time to get out safely. I convalesced for several months but unfortunately never went back to work. But those people I will never forget and it surprises me today when I do talk about these circumstances to various people, they do still talk about it even though it's nearly twenty two years ago, and still remember it to this day, so thank you to all of them.

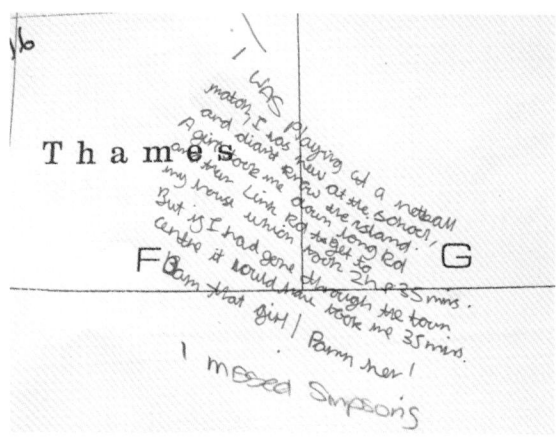

HAYSTACK CORNER:

THE BIRD MAN / PEGGY DELLER

The 'Bird Man' would wear a trilby and a grey mac, and would scatter bread for the birds. His cure for rheumatism, which he sang from Haystack Corner, included 3oz of linseed oil amongst around twenty ingredients.

Terry Hull: We used to have a bloke who used to know how to cure rheumatism. He used to sing it. Doo dee doo der doo rhe-uma-tism! And then it all rhymed. You used to walk past him and take no notice. You know... I was the only sane man on Canvey.

Peggy Deller is also remembered by many people for her work which was carried out from Haystack Corner and the grassy areas around the Paddocks. She would usually wear a red beret and would, by all accounts, reply with gusto to the taunts of local children. There was recently a message on Geoff Barsby's website from a former Canadian serviceman who was posted on Canvey, trying to contact Peggy on behalf of other servicemen who had talked about her at a recent reunion. They all remembered her fondly and wanted to send her their best wishes. After a joke from another writer that Canada Corner was in fact called that because it was at the area where Peggy used to take the Canadians, he wondered whether a plaque to remember her could be put up on Canvey– perhaps at the Paddocks where she often worked.

A few years ago 'Canada Corner', a memorial garden for the help that Canada gave during the flood, was moved from Newlands to the Paddocks, where it is now.

Arthur Reed / Roman George

TERRY HULL Arthur Reed, he could run any rabbit in the field, he could.
DAVID CAIN: Used to circle them, didn't he.
MARIE HULL: He was a bit frightening wasn't he? You know, to children. Used to scare them.
DC: I thought Arthur Reed was the most unbelievable bloke I've ever met.
TH: He died about ninety-five years old.
DC: It's only recently, he's died. But I tell you something... I remember him walking into the Haystack one day. He's got no gun, no nothing and he went, "Not bad for a days poaching." And he had these rabbits all under his coat, didn't he. And they reckon he used to be able to circle them, walk around in a circle, almost hypnotise them, then walk up to them and just pick them up. They reckon he was one of the best poachers of all time don't they? Arthur Reed. Proper snares... but they reckon he could circle a rabbit and it would almost get hypnotised like a fox would.
MOIRA CAIN: Is that what a fox does?
DC: Well, they hypnotise them. If you got headlights on a car, put yer headlights full on, the rabbit would sit in the middle of the road and that's why they get run over. They sort of get mesmerised to the whatsisname. But Arthur Reed was a good poacher. You know, you've only got to talk to people who know Arthur like. And I remember him coming in there like I say, cos he got chucked out The Haystack, didn't he?
MC: Mmmm. Quite a few times.
TH: Well, he'd want to fight you. He used to come in and he'd say, "Right, I'll have... right, five o' clock in the morning outside here". And then he'd go. It weren't no problem.
DC: But he was a cider drinker though, weren't he?
TH: No, beer.
DC: Really?
TH: Nah, he'd drink beer.
DC: I thought he drunk cider, Arthur Reed!
TH: Nah.

DC: The bloke I love was Roman George. Did you ever meet him, Roman George? Used to drink down the Commodore. He used to go in the Martinique. Used to go in there with Minty Sparkes and that, and a few of the other lads: "Hello George, how many Romans you killed today?" And he would say, "Yeah I was in the arena today and we slaughtered so many Romans." Don't you remember him? He was harmless. He was harmless but he really thought he was a real gladiator. And he was ever so smart! Proper tie!

IT WAS ESTABLISHED IN FEBRUARY 2007 AT THE LOBSTER SMACK THAT ARTHUR REED AND ROMAN GEORGE WERE IN FACT THE SAME PERSON

The painting over of 'Oz Now You Next' photographed by Stephen Bullock, 2006

CROSS OVER THE ROAD, TOWARDS FISKS ESTATE AGENTS. THE NEXT POINT OF INTEREST IS THE LEFT-SIDE WALL OF THIS BUILDING.

Oz

Now You Next
(side of Fisk's)
Jim Gray

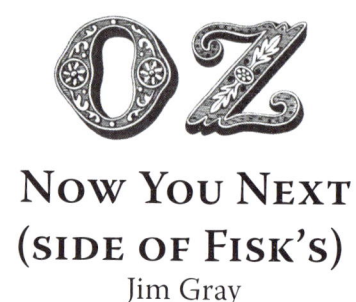

I remember looking through the window from *Grouts the Bakers* across Furtherwick Road at Pollards' wall and seeing for the first time the graffiti, 'Oz Now You Next'. It was 1971 and these words, seen from across the wooden shelves of cakes and pastries presented me with a salty and unsettling message that I barely understood. 'Oz Now You Next': the letters were painted in bold blue gloss paint in block capital letters and each ran in irregular bloody runnels. 'Oz Now You Next', a two-line poem in free verse; the first line a recognition of the present condition, the second line a near future guarantee. 'Oz Now You Next', an alien chant with w, x, y & z running through its centre. The words tickled the nape of my neck as I stood in the queue in *Grouts*.

My wife tells me that it's just paint on a wall and laughs at my 'Pseud's Corner' musings and yet the 'Oz Now You Next' graffiti was important for me as it ushered debate about youth culture, censorship and freedom of speech. Oz was an underground magazine born of the 60's hippy culture that challenged the prevailing ideology of the day and in 1971 it found itself at the centre of the longest obscenity trial in history.
John Mortimer, Q.C., representing the defendants, told the members of the jury in his opening remarks, "You will probably hear a lot about sex in this case and you may hear something about drugs. We would also like you to hear something about the basic beliefs which the people who edited that magazine share, basic beliefs with which few of us would quarrel. A genuine, and generally held, belief that racial tolerance is preferable to intolerance. That love between people is preferable to hatred. That freedom of expression is at all times preferable to censorship... It is in pursuit of those beliefs that this prosecution and this trial originates."

The offending issue was Oz No. 28, the School Kids' Issue and the indictment against the magazine's three editors included conspiring to corrupt the morals of children and young persons. An indictment that the Greek philosopher, Socrates 3000 years earlier stood on trial for owing to his refusal to uncritically accept the State's values and attitudes.

In August 1971, after five and a half weeks of argument in the Old Bailey, Oz's editors Richard Neville, James Anderson and Felix Dennis were found guilty. Neville, the magazine's main editor got fifteen months, the other two twelve and six months respectively.

So it was then that Pollard's wall, overlooking Furtherwick Park School, at the time the only secondary school on the Island, was the canvas for political protest about freedom of expression and state control and remained there, miraculously, for thirty-five years. A historical document of a time when graffiti was daubed on walls with paint brushes and motivated by political controversy. It was an education for me, I was shocked to read a grassroots message of dissent, a voice that ran counter to the mainstream media line and by the grassroots method of expressing it. This was freedom of speech in action and it gave me an appreciation of the significance of the counter-cultural youth movement and led me by the hand towards the logic of Punk.

Years later I read Tony Palmer's long unavailable *The Trials Of Oz*, a thorough account of the trial that I picked up cheap from Barnardo's on the High Street which used to be opposite the Nat West Bank. It was riveting reading; the truly interesting point that stands out is that the liberal witnesses brought forward to defend the magazine turn in a dreadful performance one after another and Mr Leary, the prosecuting Counsel dominates completely. In fact, in reading *The Trials Of Oz*, I discovered that I had moved silently towards the side of the Prosecution and had become allied to the unnamed enemy of 'Oz Now You Next'. Such are the tricks of time.

Incidentally, the sentences were later repealed weeks following the end of the trial and the indictment of conspiracy to corrupt minors has never been used since. To commemorate the 30th anniversary of the Oz trial I sent a postcard of myself leaning against the graffiti of 'Oz Now You Next' to my sister Moira, Andrew Jackson, Dave Bullock, Kevin Gardner and David Mitchell. All Canvey Island baby boomer idealists.

I'm nostalgic for a time when a young generation had an ideological position to defend. The 'Oz Now You Next' graffiti had become a historical document and proof of a politicised generation. How apt then that, when Pollards' brick wall was painted over in 2006 and the thirty-five-year-old warning was hidden, Canvey's Brave New Youth sprayed meaningless signatures across the new canvas like feral cats. Nothing to say, nothing to defend. Thinking about it, maybe 'Oz Now You Next' came true after all. The freedom to articulate dissent is lost on today's ASBO adolescent, not so much by way of direct state intervention but through ignorance.

I'm also mindful of the abuses that freedom of expression has brought. It seems that everything has not just been questioned but trivialised and debunked, and little has been put in its place. It has led to moral relativism and habitual irony where people constantly dissociate themselves emotionally from what is said. It has contributed to a breakdown in authority and it has altered childhood within the space of a generation. Was it conceivable that there would be curfew orders placed upon Canvey's teenagers thirty-five years ago? Ten years ago?

So, 'Oz Now You Next'. Daubed on a wall without irony at a time when there was an authority big enough to rail against. It was a watershed that marked a beginning and an end.

ABOVE FISKS ESTATE AGENTS THERE WAS
FORMERLY A CAFE CALLED

THE 39 CAFE
Shirley Coates

I used to go there on a Saturday when I worked in the hairdressers down the road. I used to go there on a Saturday lunchtime, and it was upstairs above the launderette that used to be there then, and one particular day I was up there and I can't remember what I actually had for lunch but I got the tomato sauce bottle, and shook it like do, and the last person hadn't put the lid on and the tomato sauce went all over a guy called Tony Wells who was in the year above me at school, and I covered him in tomato sauce.

The other story was the man who blew his hand off...

I was truanting from school, and me and my friend were down by the lake and we heard someone coming and so we hid in the bushes and we were only thirteen or fourteen, and we was hiding in these bushes waiting for these people to go past, and these two boys, my age, but they were holding hands, well to two fourteen-year-old girls, we didn't really know anything about gay people in those days, we never knew what a gay person was, well, to see two boys, we thought it was hilarious, we just sat there giggling, and the two boys heard us, and they had fireworks, and apparently they intended to light it and throw it at us as punishment, but instead this firework blew up in one boy's hand and he lost most of his hand. But I didn't know that we were the intended victims. It happened in Harvest Road, they were actually building it then, and we came along there and the ambulance was there and we stopped to say hello to the workmen to ask what happened, and they said "Oh he was playing with fireworks and it blew up in his hand", and then a long time after that I was in the 39 Café having lunch with another friend and I went over to ask him if he was ok, I didn't realise it was the same boy from down by the lake, to be honest, I didn't realise it was the person who'd walked past me, and he said "Yes it was intended for you," and I was just completely shocked, really really shocked.

CONTINUE ALONG FURTHERWICK ROAD. YOU WILL PASS THE
RIO BINGO HALL ON YOUR RIGHT

THE RIO CINEMA
Kevin Gardner

Situated in Furtherwick Road just short of the Haystack pub, the Rio was, until the later 1970s, Canvey Island's cinema.

From about 1970 to 1973 I used to go to the Rio on Saturday for the morning pictures show, normally cartoons, followed by a 'Children's Film Foundation' main feature. These were films starring kids who would stumble across a gang of ne'er-do-wells up to no good, creep up behind these blaggers, catch them at it, before running up to a local bobby for him to apprehend the gang. It was all very Scooby Doo. "Would have gotten away with blag, or drugs, or arms, diamond smuggling racket if it weren't for you kids, etc." and of course, all utter baloney, for as soon as it went dark, the place would erupt into food and drink being thrown as far as possible, either at the screen or at whoever was sitting where the Kia-Ora orange carton finished up.

The queue to get in would stretch around the back into what is now the car park; not that queuing was a problem because as soon as you saw a mate ahead in the queue, you jumped in, pretending they were holding your place.

Today, Saturday morning pictures don't exist. This era was before children's TV land. No *Swap Shop* or *Tiswas* and CFF eventually had no crooks left to catch for the police. A morning at the flicks would be the prelude to a typical Canvey Saturday. After the last rogue had been rounded up, we would pile out, go home for lunch, then if it was summer, over to King Georges Fields to play football, or winter, to the Goldmine Club on the Eastern Esplanade for their Saturday afternoon kids disco, then home for *Final Score* and *Doctor Who*.

In about 1975 the film *Stardust* came to town, starring David Essex who at the time was a major pop star. This film had an 'AA' rating (15 and over), due solely to the fact that in one scene Essex was in bed with two topless women. Had it been one girl, it might have been an 'A' certificate (12 and over) but eager to protect our morals from this outrage, the filth and the fury in society's decline, depicted in this scene, the censor had decreed that this was a life for the 16 pluses only.

No bother. Fourteen or fifteen, walk a bit broader, turn your jacket collar up, talk in a gruff voice. Piece of cake getting in for this, however, meeting with the queues was the least of our problems as patrolling the queues were teachers from my school, pulling out all those still in the third year. I was tapped on the shoulder and pulling down my jacket collar and walking a little less broad, sent packing.

I never did get in to see that film and in those days, once a film had finished its run, it was gone. No videos, DVDs and not on the box for years. Essex dies of a drug overdose at the film's finale, but that seemed irrelevant in terms of who could legally see it. I got into a couple of Bond films at the Rio with no problems, despite Roger Moore's increasing body count, with both baddies and Bond girls.

Other films I can remember seeing there were *The Battle of Britain* and *Charge of the Light Brigade*. God, they were long films, with intermissions, depicting hundreds of people getting killed. Death never bothers a censor as much sex, or even the suggestion of it. I also saw *Those Magnificent Men in their Flying Machines* and *Chitty Chitty Bang Bang* at the Rio. More films with intermissions.

I can't remember why it closed or when it became a bingo hall. Multiplexes weren't around, but I would guess that it was just a local 'fleapit' that local people grew bored of, especially with newer cinemas open in Southend. The Rio could only show one film at a time, whereas the Odeon in Southend had at least two films on two screens. The Rio couldn't take films like *Star Wars* and *Close Encounters* which we all trooped into Southend to see on bigger screens with bigger sound systems.

As the fading star in *Sunset Boulevard* observed, "I never got any smaller. The movies did." For the Rio though, she was wrong.

Detour: Thorney Bay

When you reach the sea front and the Labworth cafe, take an optional detour to the right along the sea wall, to Thorney Bay

Joan Liddiard: *If anything drifted, it would have ended up at Thorney Bay. Because that's where everything ended up. That's why it was called Dead Man's Point, because if anybody drowned they would have been washed in, and you would also get lots of debris. When my kids were about four or five we were always walking around there, it would be our regular haunt, and all round there on the sand would be hospital waste. They would put all the hospital waste on the boat, and there would be the needles and all that, but also false limbs, and my kids used to think it was wonderful! Bolting on a false leg and making out they were peg-leg and that, so yes, everything always ended up there.*

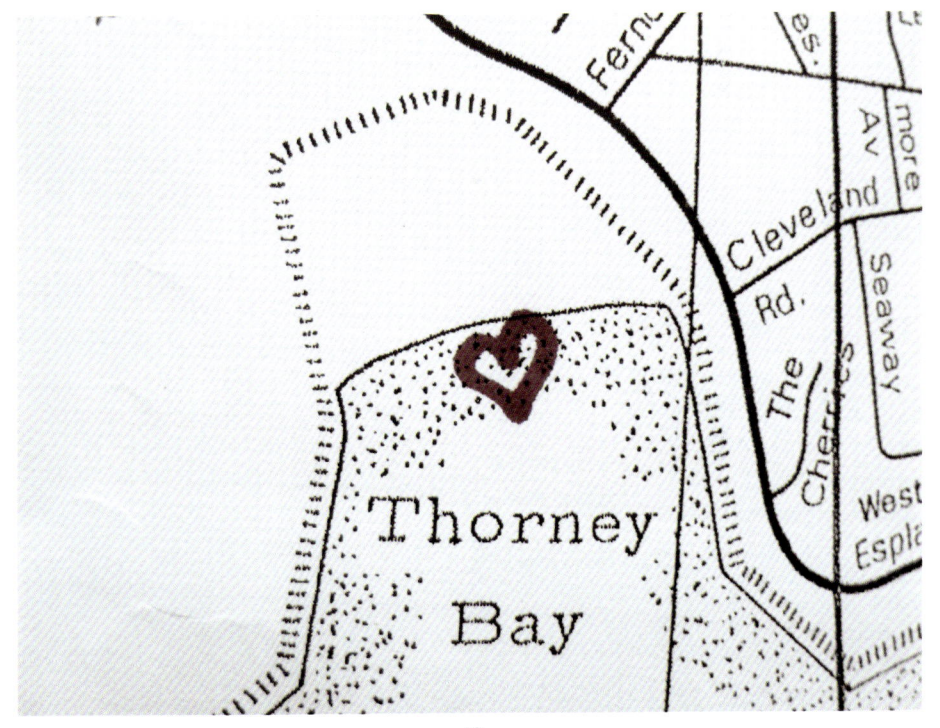

Thorney Bay
Chris Keene

Canvey Island and the Thames Estuary, is a major wintering ground for wildfowl and wading birds from all over the north of Europe. Just down here on the right we see these rocks, the old sea wall that has now disintegrated and you get parties of turnstones hunting in for small insects and things like that in the weeds around the rocks, they love to do that and then you have the expansive mud beyond there. It's a sheltered little bay here, and the birds, the wading birds, the dunlin, the redshanks, oystercatchers, curlews, they all come in here and feed at low tide. When the tide's out they can eat the invertebrates who are in the mud; it's a very rich feeding ground for them.

Now behind us we have a classic example of the ignorance of certain people who are in positions of authority, but who don't really know anything about the environment. There was a fine piece of wind-blown sand here that's been anchored by the grasses and was growing various wild flowers and even shrubs, and it was a perfect feeding ground for small birds that like to eat the seeds on the weeds, and we had some sparrows and linnets and goldfinches and green finches and we used to get kestrels hunting along here, but now you can see they've removed all of that and now we just have bare concrete. It looks like a bit like someone's front garden that's been paved over to put their car there, but of course it's completely barren for wildlife and over in the corner there the council have made this token bit of rockery which they say is environmentally friendly, but it's planted with foreign plants which will get very few insects and seeds and things like that for the birds, so as you can see there are no birds there, at the moment and I doubt very much we'll get anything there at all.

My Hedge
Irene Willis

If you're standing at Thorney Bay, if you look across the road to the bottom of the Parkway, you will see a hedge which has been untouched for about twenty years, and it's full of berries in the winter for the birds, and at dawn and dusk the sparrows tend to roost there and move around, and it's just this hive of wonderful birds. Thrushes, magpies, starlings all make so much use of it.

After you have spent time at Thorney Bay, go back along the sea wall. Go past the Labworth cafe and climb up the steps over the sea wall.

You will see the Monico pub, and next to it there is a space which sometimes has armchairs arranged as if in a living room. This is the former site of the Casino.

If you go inside the Monico you can see photographs of the Casino on the wall to your right. You may wish to stop for a drink or some food here.

The Casino

David Cain

The Casino Ballroom as I remember it was a hall where people went dancing, once a week, I think. They had big bands, like proper bands you know, proper jazz bands and things like that, and I remember looking through the door and seeing people in there: proper girls dancing, men with bow ties – proper ballroom dancing. I never went myself but later on, in later years, they still used to have it open as a dance hall and they had the Battle of the Bands up there. All the girls used to sit one side and all the blokes another side, and it was like the bravest bloke seemed to dance with the best girl that night, whoever got up.

You know I remember when the mods and rockers come down and they kicked off at the Casino one night. The police just weren't in sight and that was the real first riot. And that was the only big fight I've ever seen, down in the Casino and I was about fifteen or sixteen and I was sort of hiding in the doorway at the time and you had everybody out there. My dad I suppose. People like Terry and that, they'll remember it. Never seen anything like it.

Well, what basically used to happen was, in the summer they used to come down sit on the sea wall. All the mods and that would come down from London and over from Clacton or somewhere like that, basically. And you used to have a motorbike club, what was it? The Fifty Nine Club was it? And the Fifty Seven. They used to have different numbers these clubs, Ninety Nine Club, I suppose. They used to turn up with hats with chains on and studded belts and everything else. But I can remember them coming down one day, you could hear the motor bikes coming down and all the mods used to be on the sea wall and the rockers would be in the Monico, having a good drink-up I suppose, fighting over the girls as usual and I suppose it really did kick off. But I've never seen anything like it to this day, but it was like a war out there. Like I say, the police weren't in sight that day. All shot off. But I suppose at the end of the day, no one got stabbed. They didn't use knives or anything like that. That's the difference. That's what we're talking about. And then afterwards everybody would go and have a drink together, you know.

When you have finished at the Monico and Casino, carefully cross back over the road. If you go over to the Amusement Arcade to your right you should be able to see two horse rides outside which have an occasional soundtrack. These are the last remaining items from the Casino.

Head up the pathway to the sea wall with the Labworth on your right. Go back down the steps over the sea wall. The walk now continues along the wall all the way to the Point at the end. You will see a large piece of graffiti on the sea wall, which relates to a time some years ago when a woman on Canvey claimed to have seen a vision in her back garden.

Joan Liddiard: *It was in the 70s or early 80s, I think– and because she reckoned she had the Virgin Mary in her garden, coachloads came down. I didn't know about it at the time, although I was living here, but a friend of mine lived in her road at the time, and he said yes, they came down by the coachload.*

Fantasy
CAFE
Jayne

CKET POTATOES

Fantasy
TAKE AWAY
Fayre

Canvey Point

Continue along the sea wall pathway, which will soon turn a corner. Go right to the very end, when you turn the final corner and can see the pathway disappear.

Climb up the final set of steps and follow the sea wall along the stony pathway along the top.

When you get to the Yacht Club you will see a pathway which runs along the side, signposted as a footpath. This pathway is only accessible when the tide is out. Go along to the stile and look out to the estuary. This is Canvey Point, where the Romans used to gather salt and where an American plane crashed during the Second World War.

You are also now near the former location of Canvey's Concrete Barge.

DEREK LYNCH: *When the American plane crashed we were out there. I must have been ten or eleven, and we were catching shrimps, and we saw them coming over, then one slipped and hit the other one, and we were definitely first on the scene because the police wanted to know how we got there. They were stopping people going to the Point but we were already there. We got quite a telling off because it was still banging, you know the bullets in the fire were all going off.*

Many Canvey residents go to the Point to collect Roman artifacts, which are kept in houses all over the island. Gary Foulger has talked of how he goes out here at night to collect these objects but also to think, and how he sees his footsteps glowing with the phosphorus that is in the ground. Gary organised the retrieval of the plane from the Point and it is now at the Dutch Cottage Museum.

The Concrete Barge photographed by Steve Bullock in 2002

Canvey Concrete Barge
Canvey Point Saltings
David Bullock & Andrew Jackson

You are now standing near hallowed ground, witness to the shattered grandeur of THE Concrete Barge, the mysterious monolith that graced Canvey's coast for sixty years. This 250 ton ferro-concrete Barge, with her huge dark wooden diagonal rubbing strakes was a stunning Canvey landmark. More than that, she was a secret meeting place, an adventure playground, a lovers' rendezvous, a place of solitude – a place to get drunk. For all Canvey Islanders, The Concrete Barge simply *was*.

Various myths developed as to her origin. I remember being told she was built by a mad inventor and had never floated due to being made of concrete. Another tale is she was put there to show the Germans that Canvey 'meant business' during World War II. If so, it worked, as there is no record of any Germans landing at Canvey Point.

Research seems to confirm that Canvey's Concrete Barge was a WW2 veteran, a fuel barge which, along with a larger Mulberry Harbour concrete caisson, broke loose from the convoy during bad weather. The caisson beached off Thorpe Bay, beyond Southend Pier in the distance, and the Concrete Barge found its way to her new home on Canvey. Apparently she was bought from the War Office for one pound and brought round to Canvey Point to house a floating canoe club. During more bad storms in 1952, a year before even worse storms would cause the great flood, she was holed by her owners to prevent ramming against the sea wall. From that day onwards she rested on the sand alongside Roman ruins, a crashed Flying Fortress and a Viking ghost.

There are some 1950s pictures of the Concrete Barge in pristine showroom condition. But over the years she showed signs of her age; those majestic wooden strakes fell off one by one, sections of concrete crumbled, revealing the iron bar reinforcements, and she became covered in witty informative graffiti. In 1980, Dave, Steve Tolton and I held an impromptu gig on the barge, playing those exposed iron bars like a giant harp, and the huge iron knocker at her bow for percussion.

In the late 1960s a famous pop group made a promotional film on the concrete barge which was shown on *Top of the Pops.* This much we know, but no one can quite agree who it was. Depending on who you ask it was either The Shadows, The Tremeloes, The Spencer Davies Group, or (ahem) The Beatles. In the late 70s, Canvey legend Lew Lewis, the greatest white harmonica player in history, did a photo shoot at the barge, brandishing a knife, an axe and a shotgun, accompanied, bizarrely, by Lee Brilleaux's collie dog.

Three years ago, the unthinkable happened. On 22nd May 2003 the Concrete Barge was destroyed by the adjacent Yacht Club. What Hitler, the IRA and local vandals had failed to do, they did in one day with a couple of JCBs. Without warning, the world's most loved Concrete Barge was reduced to rubble. Protests from locals, the Heritage society, the RSPB, the PLA and Prince Charles all came too late. The Yacht Club's glib response was that the barge was an eyesore.

You may notice the Concrete Barge has not quite vanished. Her concrete hull and steel rod skeleton, draped in funeral black seaweed, emerge from the mud, sand and rocks. In 2004 I gathered a few iron bars from this site as sacred relics. They provide the chimes you hear now on this lament for THE Concrete Barge. Rest in Peace, dear old friend.

We have set up www.concretebarge.co.uk dedicated to her memory. Here you can find out more about her history, view photographs and share your memories. There are even art works and barge-related poetry.

The Concrete Barge will never be forgotten.

Continue along the sea wall path. You'll cross an access point for the creek: STOP LOOK LISTEN as it says on the sign in front of you– and cross the tracks.

You'll pass the Canvey Supply yard on your left, and a small viewing platform or break in the wall to your right. It's marked with a sign warning that it is a DESIGNATED CONFINED SPACE. You have a good view of the creek and the boats from here. As you continue you should see Kings Park, the pond and the gates of Canvey Heights in front of you. Walk down the slope and enter the park.

You have now reached

CANVEY HEIGHTS

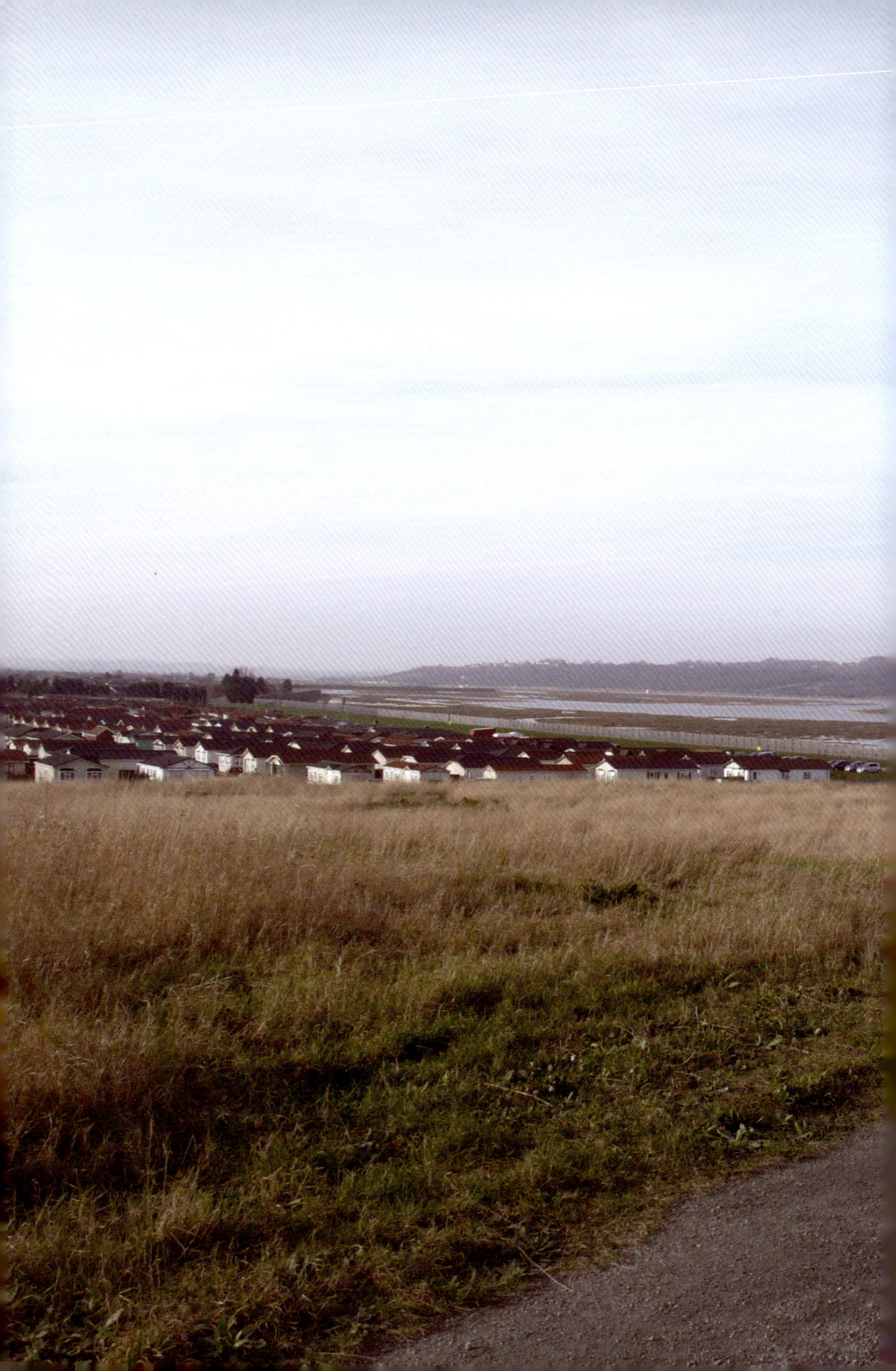

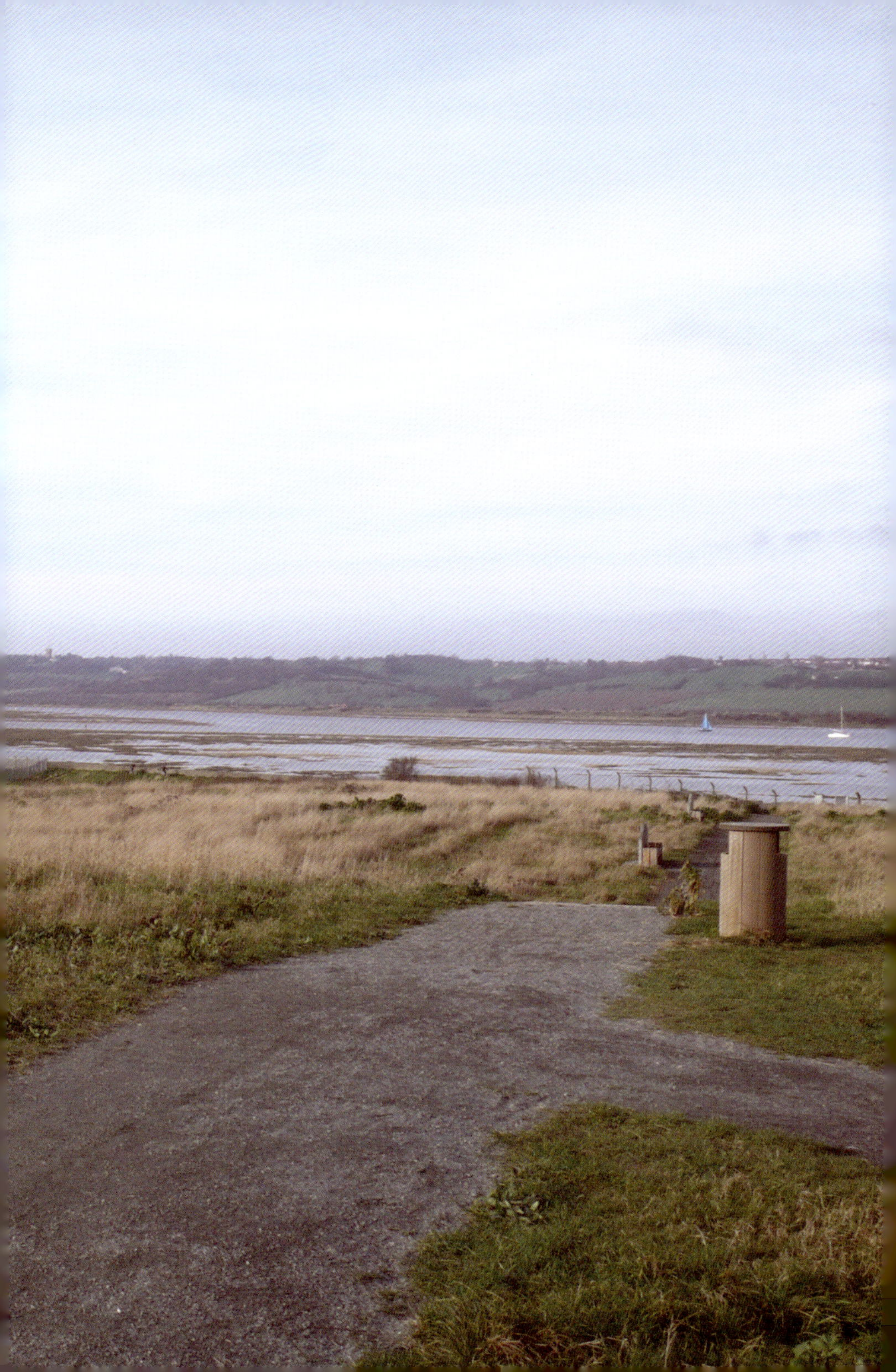

The View to Leigh
Margaret Payne

I've been asked to remember bits of my past when I half lived on Canvey and half lived in London but came every weekend and every summer holidays to Canvey, to stay with my grandparents. I lived in May Avenue and I still live there in the same bungalow, and my chosen location is the view from Canvey Heights towards Benfleet and then east to Southend because I remember when none of the present development was there and it was just fields and cows. What I remember most about where I used to stay, at Grandma's, was that it was very rural, and very basic. There was an outside toilet which had to be emptied every day. My granddad was absolutely assiduous in making sure that we didn't go out at that time, and it was taken to the top of the garden behind the roses, I believe, and I stayed for most of the summer holidays even when I was about eighteen, with my grandparents.

The road at that time was not called Tewkes Road, as it is now, but was Jarlsberg Avenue, which was a very old Dutch name as Hester had named it, and their bungalow was wooden, it was charming, basic, and always seemed to be sunny. And their wooden bungalow had an upstairs and it was reached by a outside staircase, which had a safety handrail and at the top it became a little balcony, and from there I would be able to look out with no gaps, without anything to stop the view, straight from my grandma's upstairs balcony, across the sea wall which was much lower than it is now, to Leigh and Hadleigh Castle. And running along the base of Hadleigh Castle was the railway line that went from Southend, to Benfleet and up to London, and my boyfriend lived at Leigh, and so when we made an arrangement to meet I would stand and watch the train from Leigh, past Hadleigh Castle, and I would be on the balcony, and watching it draw in, to Benfleet station, and thinking, ooh he'll be here soon, he'll be here soon, and feeling somewhat romantic about it all, and I can always remember afterwards, looking back on that and thinking, I wish I had shown to him the excitement that I felt, because I don't think I ever told anybody until now, the sort of 'Ooh lovely, he's coming' sort of feeling.

The View Towards the Creek
Chris Fenwick

I'm standing at Canvey Heights overlooking the creek, with two very contrasting views in front of me. On my left, the sea wall drops away into the interior of the island – low-lying ground which is mostly filled with 'upside-down houses'. These are Canvey's architectural speciality, built with the bedrooms downstairs and the sitting rooms upstairs, so that there's a view from the sitting room window out over the sea wall. The house I'm actually thinking of isn't just any old upside-down house– it's where my best friend Lee Brilleaux lived as a boy.

When he grew up Lee found fame as singer with Canvey Island's own chart-topping band, Dr Feelgood. He was well-known and well-respected all round the world. But to me he always remained the childhood friend with whom I used to play on the marshes. And that's the view I can see now as I look down towards the creek – the salt marshes and mud flats bordering Benfleet Creek, which separates Canvey Island from the outside world. Out there is the low, elongated shape of Long Horse Island, really just a mud bank covered in marsh plants. That was a magical treasure to Lee and me. We'd row out there and spend all day mucking about, telling tall tales and having adventures in the rickety old camp we built.

Later on we made sorties over to the Essex mainland, which rises in a high slowing cliff beyond the creek; and we also ventured across the Thames estuary to explore the shores of North Kent– foreign country to Canvey Island lads in those days. But it was these Canvey marshes that were always our favourite playground. Lee drew a wonderful pirate map of Long Horse Island and the marshes, and I've got that map hanging in my house today.

Lee died of lymphoma in 1994. Some of his friends and family brought his ashes down in a boat and scattered them in Benfleet Creek. That wasn't quite according to the law. But we thought it was right that he should rest here, along the creeks and marshes that he loved so much when he and I were Canvey boys and best mates together.

Benfleet

Wharf

Avocet Island

Black Skull Island

Puffin

Frenchman's Inlet

Whimbrel Island

Curlew Is.

Sandpiper Creek

Tewkes Creek

Flintlock Is.

RUM

Lee Brilleaux's 'pirate map' of the creek (1966)
reproduced by kind permission Chris Fenwick

Lunch at the Tip
Barbara Taylor

In the early sixties the Young Conservatives one year helped in the organising of the Canvey Island Carnival. It was decided that instead of calling it a Carnival that year it would be a Festival and they would have a Festival Princess, in place of a Carnival Queen.

Well, I was delighted when, after an eliminating event held at the then Rio Cinema, I was chosen to be the Festival Princess. The actual Festival was a lovely day and we had a horse-drawn carriage instead of the usual float, and a disco in the evening. At that time, the local authority was beginning to reclaim the ground at the site of the rubbish tip and to publicise this, it was decided to have a lunch there. So there we were, dignitaries, Festival organisers, the Press and me, complete with crown, etc. all having lunch on trestle tables set up on the site of a rubbish tip! It was different, to say the least.

A short time afterwards someone sent me a photograph of me and a nice young reporter, sitting on one of the cars having a chat. I wonder what happened to him, he was rather nice!

Fond Memories of Canvey Tip
Janet Penn

On a Sunday afternoon in the spring of 1993 or 94 I found myself sitting in the Castle Point Mobile Volunteer Bureau's vehicle (an old ambulance) outside Canvey Tip. Why was I there? I later asked myself that very question.

As a founder member of the Volunteer Bureau I was asked if I could help out with the Mayor's Charity Walk. Every spring the Mayor has a walk round part of the sea wall starting and finishing back at Waterside Sports Centre, to raise money for their chosen Charity. As my children were being sponsored to join in the walk I said, "Yes what can I do to help?"

They needed me to sit in the Mobile Volunteer Bureau's vehicle parked outside the tip during the walk offering drinks and help to anyone that needed it. I thought, "I can do that no problem". Famous last words!

The vehicle was duly parked with me on board at the gates to the tip. I had studying to do so was quite happy sitting there reading until the walkers started to call in. After the last of the walkers had passed me the weather started to get worse. I had a while to wait before anyone would be in a position to collect me.

I was not worried at first but as the hours ticked by and the rain fell and the wind howled I began to feel I had been forgotten. If only we had mobiles in those days. After several hours not seeing a soul with no toilet, unable to drive with a long walk in the wind and rain as the only alternative I was beginning to panic. At last someone arrived.

Yes, they had all forgotten me. They had all been at Waterside eating and drinking in the dry, out of the wind and *they had toilets*. Not giving me a thought. This included my children, I might add.

Soon after the tip was closed for good, later being transformed into Canvey Heights, I just hope my first visit is less stressful.

Canvey Heights Country Park was made by capping Newlands landfill site and opened in 2003. Janet Penn first went to Canvey Heights at the inaugural meeting of the Rendezvous Walking Club in December 2006.

A Walk
Valerie Lynch

Walk from Canvey Rugby Club Car Park on Spovervelt Road. Turn left out of the car park, again turn left into Kellington Road. Take the grassy slope up on to the top of the sea wall. Look out towards Benfleet on your left and you will see at the highest point Benfleet water tower at the top of the Essex Way/Benfleet Road. Follow the wall towards the right in the direction of Canvey Heights. Look out across the saltings to Benfleet Downs and Hadleigh Castle. Over Tewkes and Benfleet Creeks below the castle you will see the remains of an old jetty. Many birds visit these saltings: herons, egrets, brent geese, Canada geese, plover, mallards and many gulls to mention a few. Sometimes in summer when the tide is low you can see the odd seal basking in the sun on the mudflats. Walking further along you can see Two Tree Island, moorings and across to Leigh-on-Sea.

As you approach Kings site the Estuary opens out and you can see across to Southend and on a clear day the pier. You reach access on your right to a counter sea wall (that abuts Nordland Road). This leads to the front entrance of Kings and the bus stop.

If you continue alongside the main sea wall, where Kings bungalows end, to your right, is a small footpath that leads to the front entrance (on your left) of Canvey Heights. You can continue along the main sea wall through the narrow fence path to the creekside entrance to the Canvey Heights park. Take in the view from the top or sit and rest at the picnic area.

If you choose not to visit the Heights, continue along the maintained footpath alongside the creek which encircles Canvey Heights, look across and you will eventually see boat and yacht clubs and moorings across Small Gains Creek and Saltings. Canvey Heights entrance is on your right when the footpath ends, or continue left on top of the sea wall, and you will pass the Boat Club (Halcons) on the Mississippi barge and Canvey Supply yard on your right. Eventually reaching the Island Yacht Club, look straight out and you will see a small natural footpath leading out to Canvey Point. Only attempt this footpath when the tide is going out, as on high tides it can get a little wet. The view is so open, right out to the Point. You can also continue around the sea wall. When you turn sharp right, the Estuary is much wider and you can look across to the Kent coast and see the Isle of Grain and All Hallows in the distance. Eventually you reach Shell Beach, the Canvey Amusement Arcades, Labworth Beach and Café/Restaurant and onto Thorney Bay beach. It is best if you can walk as a group and leave cars at the Rugby Club or Thorney Bay car park, or for the shorter walk the Rugby Club and Canvey Heights or the Island Yacht club. Looking out from the Sea Wall across to Kent you will see many container ships, ferries, sailing and motor boats.

Around Canvey Heights: Tewkes Road

George Beecham

Most of my walks I use as a training spin, because I do race walking. Living in Tewkes Road is very convenient for me, because I can go 100 yards down the road to pick up the sea wall, and I can either go eastward out towards Kings Camp, right the way round the sea wall, up past Small Gains Creek, right back, I can either carry along there and go right along the sea wall and then come back up May Avenue, or I can cut across and come back up the tip road, or Small Gains, and come back through Small Gains. Alternatively, I can either go up to the top of Tewkes Road, down either through May Avenue and back on the sea wall and do the walk in reverse. Both ways is a good walk because it's very interesting. There's interesting scenery all the way round, you have the Hadleigh Downs, looking out, on my left if I go out on the eastward walk, or if I go on the westward way and come back, I have the whole of the sea front, looking out towards the Point, and it's quite an enjoyable walk. Alternatively, there's walks all round Canvey, and it's a beautiful place for me to go walking, there's plenty of interest. But it's quite flat, that's the only problem for me, if I want to do altitude training I have to go to Benfleet, but Canvey Heights now has given me some incentive to do a bit of hill walking up Canvey Heights.

Derek Lynch

Dad built the bungalow next door, that was- well, we came down in '35 so presumably it must have been – I was born in '33 so it must have been '34, '35... I don't know how much of a rush it was to build it. I did have some photos but I think they were all lost in the floods. We used to have a big old bell tent we used to stay in when Dad was building, and there were five houses in this road. There was Margaret Bragg's grandfather, he was down the bottom on the left, there was Ronnie Cornell who was opposite, then there was Mr Galvin, up the top and David Cown, and all the rest was fields, and dad had a couple of goat sheds and chicken runs here. I used to moan a bit when I come home from school and mum would say, "You've got to go out and cut the grass." We used to go out with a scythe, and you couldn't tell between roads and fields, it was just all grass.

Dad worked with an old chap that they called Jersey Bert, and he used to cut the briar off the wild roses and push it down the rabbit warrens, and twist and turn it and he'd say, "No, no there's nothing down there," and he'd try another one and he'd say, "Yes there's one here," and he'd wind it up and it used to wind all the fur of the rabbit up then he pull it out and the poor old rabbit was struggling and he'd pick it up and go 'bonk' on the head. I think that was the silent way of poaching, there was no noise over the fields, and I think Dad used to do the same with him.

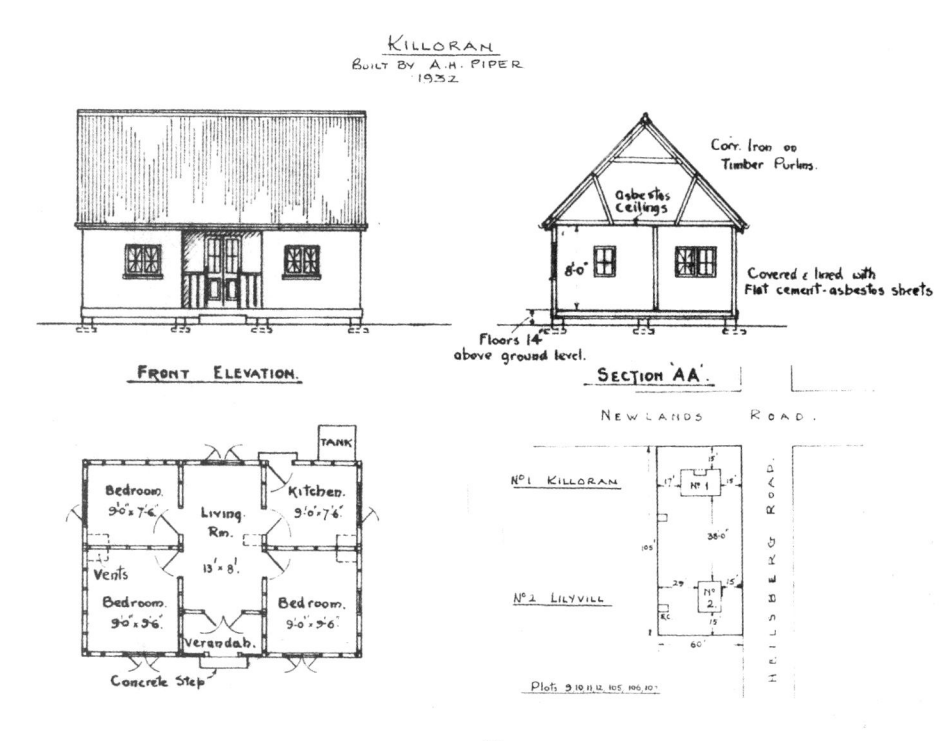

Newlands Park, Amada and Killoran
Alan Piper

Early in the 1920s the fields of "Sunken Marsh" were divided up and offered for sale at £5 a plot, under the more romantic name of Newlands Park. Arthur Piper Snr. bought six plots necessary for a dwelling, on the corner of Newlands Road and Jarlesburge (renamed Tewkes). Over the next ten years, working at odd times as money would allow, "Amada" was built and the Piper Family came to Canvey from Ilford.

The large timber-framed, asbestos-clad, veranda'ed bungalow became a retirement home during the war. Helped by a young Derek Lynch, the large garden was practically self-sufficient, which gave rise to vegetable pilfering in the district. With "Amada" at the hub, neighbours formed a vigilante army, having a hand bell to raise the alarm. The culprit was found to be a local greengrocer. "Amada" again centred in the incident of a large Alsatian dog which terrorised the neighbourhood by jumping the low picket fences and attacking people in their gardens. The dog was chased and in retreat half a brick was thrown at it. The brick missed the dog, missed the fence and went clean across the road to penetrate the neighbour's asbestos wall and land on the kitchen table.

Arthur Piper Jnr. wanted a place of his own and built "Killoran" (named after a Tea Clipper), on the corner of Newlands and Heilsberg. Eager to recoup some money, he was pleased to gain a holiday let to a chap from London, which ended in tragedy. On the last day he committed suicide and was found gassed. He had taken the let to spy on his estranged wife and her lover, and had found it all unbearable.

Alan Piper and Derek Lynch first met at the January 2007 Rendezvous Club and through their conversation realised that Derek had worked for Alan's family

FOOTPATHS OF CANVEY

Valerie Lynch

You see a lot of our footpaths are disappearing, into people's gardens and into Kings Camp I'm afraid, and it's really sad. I used to work for the council, in planning, and I tried so hard to get them to do something about the footpaths over this area, because they were gradually being closed off and we were being denied access.

There was always a footpath all the way round the perimeter of Kings Camp, and one that used to go through the middle. There's a gate there that they lock now, well, you used to be able to walk across there– it's a shame, I mean I've got letters going back to maybe the early 80s, where I tried to get Essex to do something to preserve the footpaths. Even little alleyways that I used to walk the children up to Leigh Beck school, they've all been taken into people's gardens, you know, short cuts that we used to use.

At the bottom of this sea wall, people have taken out their gardens. We always used to be able to walk at the bottom of the sea wall right the way up to Kings Camp but they've all brought their gardens out so you have to walk along the top now. I even had a search done, I probably have search documents still, detailing the width of the piece of ground that didn't belong to anyone over there but now is in people's gardens.

Miscellaneous
Tony Buckmaster's caravan

David Cain: He was a very good artist.
Terry Hull: But where did he streak though?
DC: He's done it for charity out of an aeroplane... and a sky dive. They weren't going to let him do it...
DC: He was on the Terry Wogan show.
TH: You know who come round to see him in his caravan? Who had the TV show in the morning, got the sack, that MP.
DC: Who was that?
Moira Cain: Oh Kilroy!
TH: Kilroy, yeah... it was in the News of the World. He went round to interview him in his caravan.
DC: But the queen weren't amused, was she? Ha ha ha...
TH: No, definitely not.
MC: Was it Ascot or Derby day?
DC: What he done, where the winning line was... and that's true that is, you know... so where the Queen was, where her box is, he decides then to rip his clothes off and run down the track following the horses in. I would actually imagine that must have been about 71. Something round about that time... Cos I was in the army. I'm sure I was in the army at that time.
TH: Because his father was the only bookie running on Canvey... when there was no bookmakers.
MC: He used to take my Dad's bet. In the Kynochs. He'd meet my Dad every Saturday and he'd say, "Put any money on, Jim?"
TH: That's it. Certain places of the street he'd be on and all, certain times.
DC: He painted Marilyn Monroe on his caravan wall.
MC: A mural.
DC: He did and all. With her dress blowing up and everything else. And he done these three horses. And like I say, he can paint and all. Anyway, but what he didn't realise, obviously, cos they're not on canvas, they're painted on the caravan. So he wanted to get a set... you know like to cut the side of the caravan. Well, so he said to me and a few other of the boys, "Do you reckon we could cut the painting off the walls?" He wanted to keep them. And do it properly. And er... they crushed it. Ha ha, they crushed the caravan. Really upset.

Miscellaneous

Postal Routes

The postmen and women of Canvey organise the deliveries by dividing the town up into Walks, some of which are taken on by the same postman for years while others are swapped around. In 1967 there were twenty-one 'walks'. In 2007 there are forty-three.

Just a few decades ago there were only two or three houses per street, and as there were no numbers the postmen would have to remember house names in order to correctly deliver the post.

Miscellaneous

ACE-HI
AROD DEWAN
BEELIGH
CAMILLA
CASTLE VIEW
CREEK HOUSE
DELFZUL
DIX COVE
DI BOVILLE
FARHAN
GREAT RUSSELL HEAD
HAPPY DAYS
HOMESTEAD
ITLDU
KINFAUNS

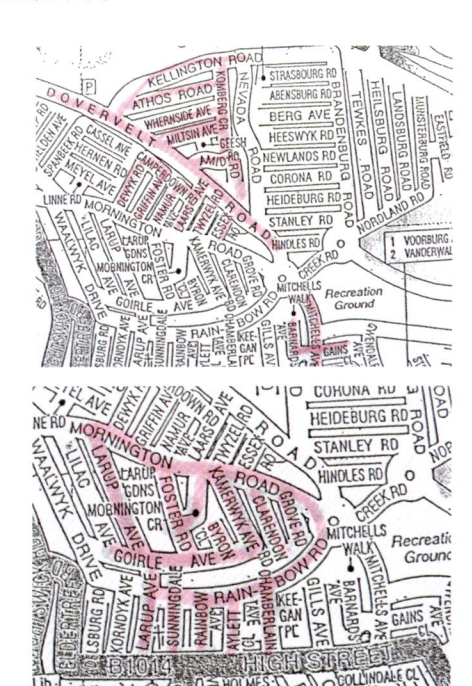

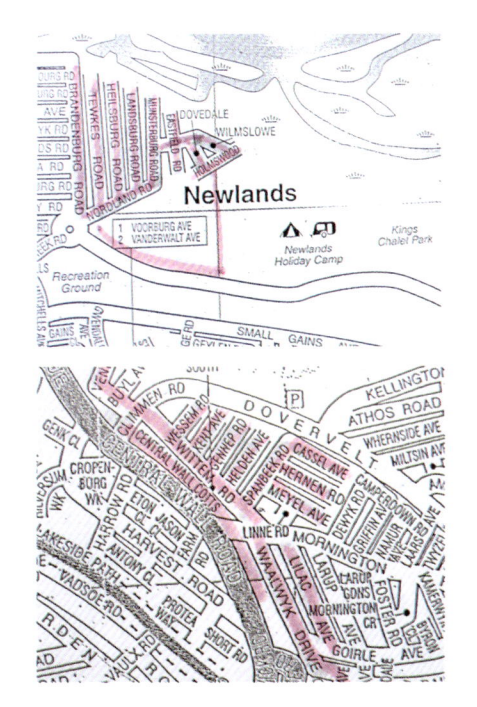

KYNANCE
LACHLAN
PANDORA'S BOX
PIGGY IN THE MIDDLE
NEWLANDS
RHY HALL
ROSE COTTAGE
ROSEBURY VILLA
RUSSELL HOUSE
SEA BREEZE
SWEYN
THIRSK
TREE LODGE
THE WILDERNESS
WISE

images: postal routes from the Sorting Office

Miscellaneous

THE RENDEZVOUS CLUB

Est. 2006
Prop. L.H. Harrison

CANVEY HEIGHTS
CANVEY ISLAND
ESSEX

THE CLUB WITH
NO RESTRICTIONS

MEETS ON THE FIRST SUNDAY
OF EVERY MONTH AT 2PM
AT THE GATES OF CANVEY HEIGHTS

*All welcome to enjoy the views
and to partake in conversation with
other members*

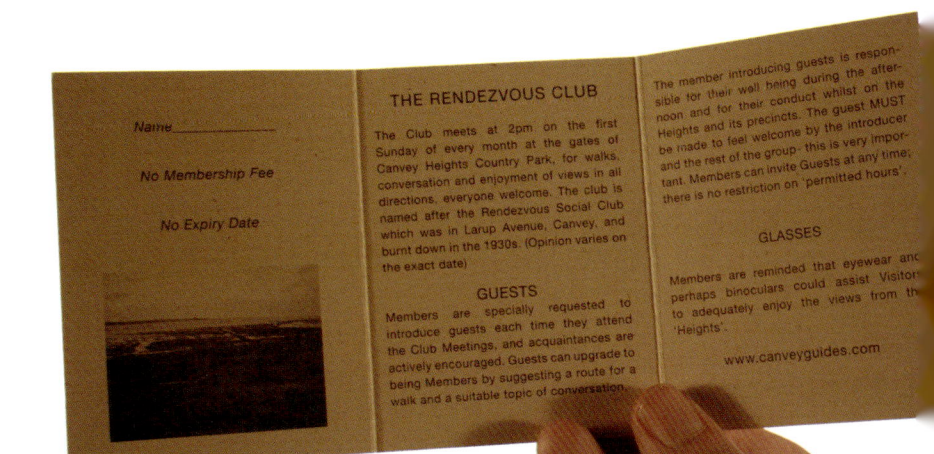

Name_____

No Membership Fee

No Expiry Date

THE RENDEZVOUS CLUB

The Club meets at 2pm on the first Sunday of every month at the gates of Canvey Heights Country Park, for walks, conversation and enjoyment of views in all directions, everyone welcome. The club is named after the Rendezvous Social Club which was in Larup Avenue, Canvey, and burnt down in the 1930s. (Opinion varies on the exact date)

GUESTS
Members are specially requested to introduce guests each time they attend the Club Meetings, and acquaintances are actively encouraged. Guests can upgrade to being Members by suggesting a route for a walk and a suitable topic of conversation.

The member introducing guests is responsible for their well being during the afternoon and for their conduct whilst on the Heights and its precincts. The guest MUST be made to feel welcome by the introducer and the rest of the group - this is very important. Members can invite Guests at any time; there is no restriction on 'permitted hours'.

GLASSES
Members are reminded that eyewear and perhaps binoculars could assist Visitors to adequately enjoy the views from the 'Heights'.

www.canveyguides.com

MISCELLANEOUS

Canvey Carnival photographed by Andrew Jackson c.1992

THEMED WALKS

NOSTALGIA (carried out by the Rendezvous Club on December 3rd 2006) via the Transport Museum and other places that may inspire nostalgia.

PRIVATE PROPERTY (carried out by the Rendezvous Club on January 7th 2007) via Kings Park Village, the Yacht Club, the Canvey Club, the Corner Club, the Kynochs Club (now closed).

RUMOURS (Carried out by the Rendezvous Club on February 4th 2007) via the sites of famous Canvey rumours.

CEREMONY via the route of the Canvey Carnival and the Lee Brilleaux Memorial walk.

FAILED PROJECTS via the site of Hester's Tower, the Jetty, Radio Tower.

LOST BUILDINGS via the Casino, the Lighthouse,

ROMANCE via sites of romantic encounters or places inspiring romantic thoughts.

Miscellaneous

Canvey Island Heritage Centre

St Katherines Church
The Church Yard
Canvey Road
Canvey Island
Essex SS8

Opening times: some weekends when exhibitions are on, or by appointment. To check or to make an appointment telephone Rosemary on 01268 694317

Miscellaneous

The Viewing Tower

Frederick Hester, who initiated the big move to Canvey from London, built a viewing tower in the Winter Gardens. The purpose of the tower was to enable prospective buyers to see plots of land available for sale. The landscape of Canvey could be viewed from above, ready to be divided up and sold off. The interested parties would arrive on a purpose-built monorail and afterwards would be given a dinner, often chicken. The monorail is now in many pieces, kept in museums, people's houses and gardens. Some of its sections are likely to be buried in the ground at the Winter Gardens on the west of the island.

Hester went bankrupt in 1905. A man from London bought the top bungalow section; the rest of the tower was demolished after being declared unsafe in 1909 when local people started taking sections of the bottom for firewood.

Below is the probable location of the tower, as decided by Dave and Steve Bullock and Margaret Payne in 2006.

Miscellaneous

Further reading

www.canveyisland.org.uk
Dave Bullock's great website including old photographs and further walks around Canvey.

www.concretebarge.co.uk
Dave Bullock & Andrew Jackson's memorial site for the Concrete Barge.

www.canveyislandhistory.com
Geoff Barsby's history site including discussion board for ex-pats and locals. Geoff Barsby also has many books available of his collection of photographs.

Canvey Island; A History by Robert Hallmann, Phillimore & Co. Ltd 2006

With many thanks to the following for guided tours, interviews, and other assistance:

Geoff Barsby, George Beecham, Dave Blackwell, Arthur Brownley, Tony Buckmaster, Dave Bullock, Steve Bullock, David Cain, Moira Cain, Kate Clayton, Geoff Coates, Shirley Coates, Mary Dallas, Barry Dixey, Roger Esgrove, Chris Fenwick, Doris Flaherty, Gary Foulger, Kevin Gardner, Bob 'The Brush' Gibbons, Jim Gray, Robert Hallmann, Sue Hampson, Nicholas Horne, Ray Howard, Terence Hull, Marie Hull, Andrew Jackson, Alison Kaye, Chris Keene, Joan Liddiard, Derek Lynch, Valerie Lynch, Peter May, Vicki Merrick, David and Madeleine Offley, Keith Patten, Marion Patten, Margaret Payne, Janet Penn, Sheila Penn, Alan Piper, Richard Powell, John Pring, Emily Redgate, Jean and Reg Reed, George and Grace Scantlebury, Les and Sylvia Skelley, Graham Stevens, Barbara Taylor, David and Jessica Thorndike, Ann Walsh, Irene Willis, pupils in Applied Arts at Castle View School, and all the other walkers at the Rendezvous Club.

Thanks to the following organisations:
2nd Hand Rose, The Canvey Club, Canvey Heritage Centre, Canvey Library, Canvey Sorting Office, Castle Point Council, Castle Point Transport Museum, Cisca House Senior Citizens Association, Fisks Estate Agents, The Monico & The Oysterfleet Hotel.

Special thanks to Jo Baxendale, Geoff and Shirley Coates, Bob & Roberta Smith and all at Commissions East.